SHE MADE
A MONSTER

*How Mary Shelley
Created Frankenstein*

By Lynn Fulton

Illustrated by Felicita Sala

Alfred A. Knopf   New York

To my family —L.F.

To Elisabetta —F.S.

✳ ✳ ✳

ACKNOWLEDGMENTS
Many thanks to Julia Maguire, and to Elena Giovinazzo and Larissa Helena
at Pippin Properties, for helping to make this story into a book.

THIS IS A BORZOI BOOK PUBLISHED BY ALFRED A. KNOPF

Text copyright © 2018 by Lynn Fulton
Jacket art and interior illustrations copyright © 2018 by Felicita Sala

Visit us on the Web! rhcbooks.com

Educators and librarians, for a variety of teaching tools, visit us at RHTeachersLibrarians.com

Library of Congress Cataloging-in-Publication Data is available upon request.
ISBN 978-0-525-57960-1 (trade) — ISBN 978-0-525-57961-8 (lib. bdg.) — ISBN 978-0-525-57962-5 (ebook)

The text of this book is set in 19-point Nicolas Cochin.
The illustrations were created using watercolor, ink, and colored pencil.

MANUFACTURED IN CHINA
September 2018
10 9 8 7 6 5 4 3 2 1

First Edition

*T*wo hundred years ago, on a wild, stormy night, in a beautiful house on the shores of Lake Geneva in Switzerland, a young woman named Mary sat at her dressing table. She and her friends were staying in the house for the season, visiting Lord Byron, the famous English poet. Mary could hear the others still talking downstairs while she brushed her hair by candlelight, thinking of stories: stories she'd read, stories she'd heard, stories she wanted to tell.

For Mary wanted to become a writer.

Her dear friend Percy Shelley, who would soon be her husband, was a poet, and Mary herself came from a family of writers. All around her she felt the power of words, and she hoped that someday she too would write something important. Something that would hit the world like a bolt of lightning splitting the night sky.

But for now, she only wanted to write a ghost story.

It had all begun when the friends had read aloud from a book of frightening tales, entertaining each other through the rainy days and nights. Lord Byron had declared: "We should each write a ghost story! In a week, we will see who has written the best one."

The week would be up tomorrow.
The men had already finished their
stories: tales of bloodthirsty vampires
and vengeful ghosts. "Of course,
Byron is sure the best one will be
his," Mary thought now. "He is
an excellent poet, after all . . . but
so arrogant!"

Yet try as she might, Mary had
found no way to begin her story.

The clock struck midnight. Mary put
down her hairbrush and tiptoed into the
hall. Over the howling wind, she could
hear her friends talking about the latest
scientific experiments, their favorite topic.
Percy's voice thundered up the stairs.
"Electricity!" he was saying. "Galvani
used it to make a dead frog kick its legs!"

Dashing back to her room, Mary felt a shiver creep over her. She remembered hearing as a young girl about an even more ghastly experiment. A scientist made a corpse move using electricity. Mary had shuddered as she listened, clinging to her father's leg. She had been only six years old.

To erase that terrible image from her mind, Mary opened her locket and looked at the tiny portrait of her mother, Mary Wollstonecraft.

She'd died when Mary was a baby. As a girl, Mary learned the alphabet by tracing the letters on her mother's tombstone.

When she was older, she read everything her mother had written: stirring words about democracy and the rights of women, words that sparked courage and inspiration in many, but anger and outrage in many others.

"Women the equals of men? What a monstrous thought!" people had said about her mother's ideas. And for Mary Wollstonecraft to *write* them was even more monstrous. Women were not supposed to have ideas of their own, let alone publish them!

Now Mary snapped her locket shut. She wanted to prove that her mother was right! A woman's writing *could* be just as important as a man's.

Downstairs, the men's voices grew louder and more excited.

"To give life to lifeless matter will be the ultimate triumph!"

"Man will conquer nature and make her give up the secret!"

Mary shook her head as she listened. "Nature might have very good reasons for keeping her secrets," she thought. "Besides, what would happen to that 'lifeless matter' once someone had given it life?" The men did not seem to care. They only asked if something *could* be done—never if it *should*.

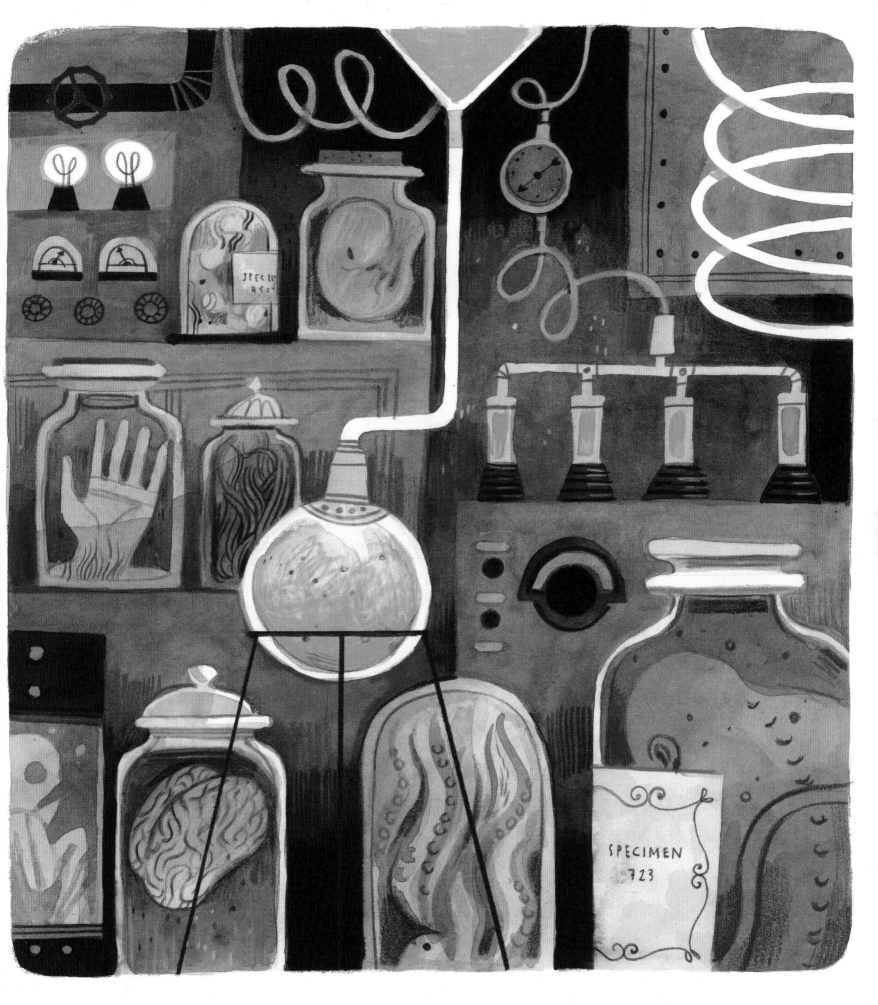

Thunder rumbled in the distance, and the rain beat harder against the window. Mary watched the wax drip down her candle. Now she could hear the others saying good night and stepping softly up the stairs.

She thought of ghosts and vampires.
She thought of monsters.
She thought of loneliness.
The night was passing, and she still didn't have a story.

A flash of lightning illuminated the room, and Mary jumped as her reflection peered back at her from the mirror, pale and strange, like something dead restored to life.

"Wouldn't it be terrifying to see such a creature?" she mused. "Or perhaps more terrifying, to *be* such a creature. . . ."

Mary got into bed and stared up into the darkness.

The house by the lake was still. The wind shrieked over the eaves, but only Mary was awake to hear it.

She let the booming thunder fill her head.

She closed her eyes to the bursts of lightning.

But she did not sleep. . . .

Instead, as if in a dream, she saw a huge form lying on a table. It was a man, yet not a man. It had a hideous, scarred face.

She saw a young student anxiously bending over the form with a candle. He had achieved his ambition—he had discovered nature's secret and given life to the creature on the table.

But now he was afraid.

He did not know what to do. He dropped the candle, covered his face with his hands, and ran away, hoping the ember of life he had sparked would die out. . . .

And suddenly, lying in her bed with the curtains shut, Mary felt as if *she* was the young creator. She felt as if she'd run to her room to cower under the sheets, trying not to think of the terrible thing she'd created. Trying not to think of it coming to find her. . . .

She trembled as she imagined a hand—
huge, gray, and twisted—appearing through
the bed curtains.

She saw the curtains part. The creature
stared down at her with bulging yellow eyes.
What did it want from her?!

Mary gasped and sat up in bed. She ripped open the curtains . . . and recognized her own room in the moonlight. All was familiar and ordinary. There was no monster.

There was only her imagination.

Her heart pounded, but she was happy.

She had found her story.

AUTHOR'S NOTE

Mary Shelley was twenty years old when *Frankenstein; or, The Modern Prometheus* was published in 1818. At first, only five hundred copies were printed. But soon all of England was talking about the dreadful tale of a man who built a monster from dead bodies. And to think it was written by a young woman! Ladies were scandalized and gentlemen were scornful, but everyone was reading it. As early as 1823, the novel was adapted for the stage. "Lo and behold, I found myself famous!" Mary wrote after seeing a performance. The first film of *Frankenstein* was produced in 1910, and since then, dozens more film, stage, radio, and TV adaptations of the book have been made.

In her introduction to the 1831 edition of *Frankenstein*, Mary tells how the chilling tale of Victor Frankenstein and his monster was born. Her account of the summer of 1816 on Lake Geneva includes the stormy weather, Lord Byron's ghost-story challenge, and her "waking dream" of "the pale student of unhallowed arts kneeling beside the thing he had put together."

Mary doesn't mention Mary Wollstonecraft in the 1831 introduction, but it seemed important to include her famous mother in the thoughts I imagined Mary might have had as *Frankenstein* was forming in her subconscious. I also added a deadline to the ghost-story challenge, making it more like a contest. And finally, I put the entire group of friends under one roof at Byron's Villa Diodati—actually, Mary, Percy, and Mary's stepsister were staying at a smaller villa nearby.

Mary Shelley's *Frankenstein* is not the same as the story most people know from the movies. Unlike the square-headed Hollywood monster with bolts in his neck, the creature in Mary's book can speak, and even read. He is lonely and longs to be part of a family, but because of his frightening appearance, he is hated and rejected by everyone, even his creator. When we envision Frankenstein's creature only as the inarticulate, raging monster of stage and screen, we lose sight of Mary's message that hatred and prejudice can turn something innocent into something murderous.

Even though it began in response to a ghost-story challenge, *Frankenstein* is, of course, not exactly a ghost story. For, just like Victor Frankenstein, Mary Shelley was creating something new—the kind of story that today we call science fiction. Whenever you read a book or see a movie about a scientist who goes too far, inventing something that becomes dangerous and uncontrollable, remember that it all began with *Frankenstein*. The monster Mary made lives on in our imaginations, just as vividly as he came into hers that stormy night, two hundred years ago.

Sources

Seymour, Miranda. *Mary Shelley*. London: Grove Press, 2000.

Shelley, Mary. *Frankenstein*. London: Penguin, 1992.

creature in Mary's book can speak, and even read. He is lonely and longs to be part of a family, but because of his frightening appearance, he is hated and rejected by everyone, even his creator. When we envision Frankenstein's creature only as the inarticulate, raging monster of stage and screen, we lose sight of Mary's message that hatred and prejudice can turn something innocent into something murderous.

Even though it began in response to a ghost-story challenge, *Frankenstein* is, of course, not exactly a ghost story. For, just like Victor Frankenstein, Mary Shelley was creating something new—the kind of story that today we call science fiction. Whenever you read a book or see a movie about a scientist who goes too far, inventing something that becomes dangerous and uncontrollable, remember that it all began with *Frankenstein*. The monster Mary made lives on in our imaginations, just as vividly as he came into hers that stormy night, two hundred years ago.

SOURCES

Seymour, Miranda. *Mary Shelley*. London: Grove Press, 2000.
Shelley, Mary. *Frankenstein*. London: Penguin, 1992.